WORLD AROUND US

Illustrated
By Lera House

CLEVER
·Publishing·

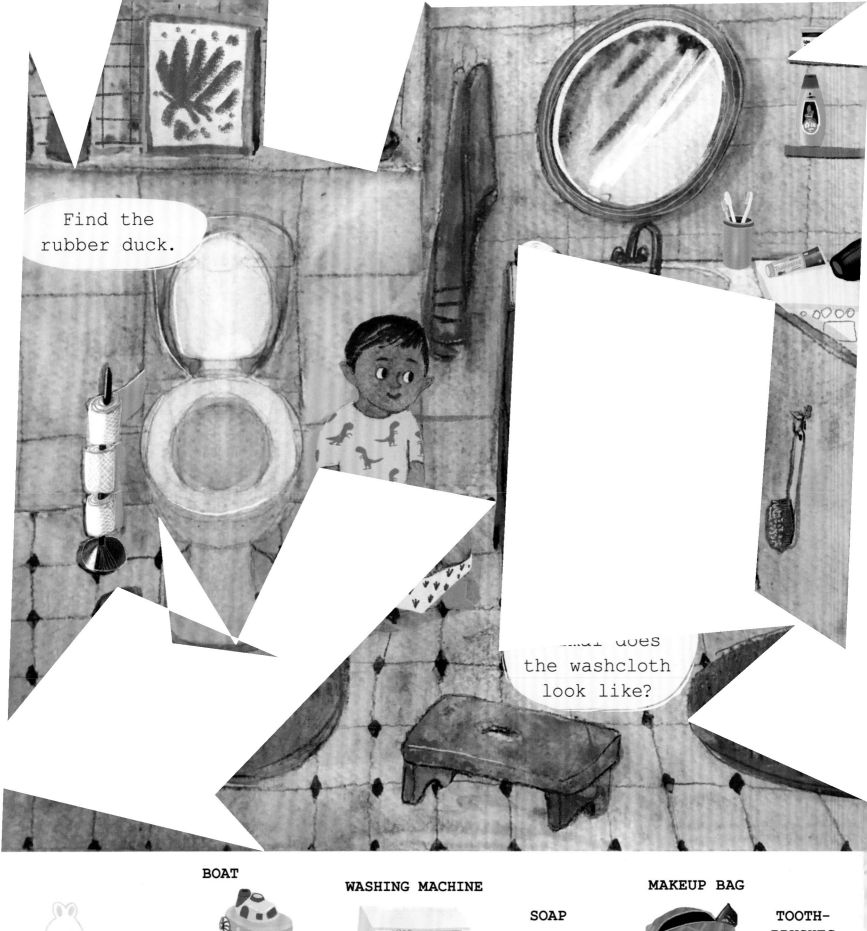

Find the rubber duck.

...at does the washcloth look like?

WASHCLOTH

DOG

BOAT

CUP

WASHING MACHINE

SOAP

TOOTHPASTE

JAR OF CREAM

MAKEUP BAG

TOOTH-BRUSHES

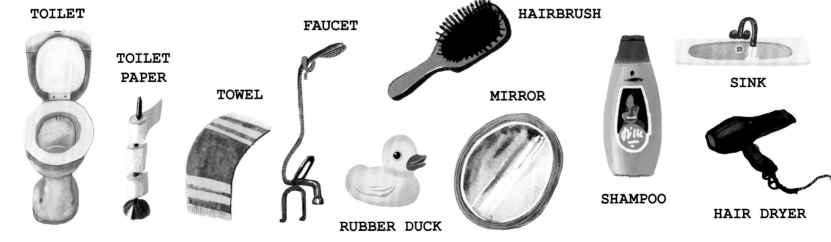

TOILET

TOILET
PAPER

FAUCET

HAIRBRUSH

TOWEL

MIRROR

SINK

RUBBER DUCK

SHAMPOO

HAIR DRYER

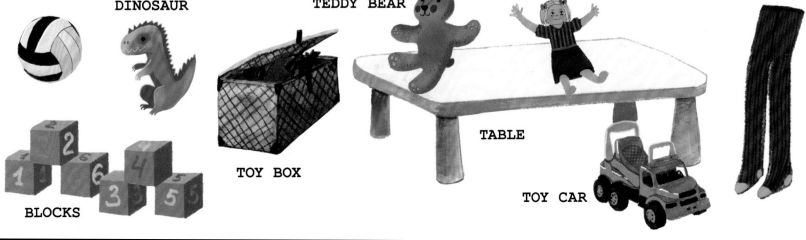

BALL

DINOSAUR

TEDDY BEAR

DOLL

TIGHTS

BLOCKS

TOY BOX

TABLE

TOY CAR

BUTTERFLY

BUSH

CAP

WHEELBARROW

RAKE

DOG

SNAIL

HOSE

HAT

SHOVEL

WATERING CAN

Which vegetables are in the wheelbarrow?

TROWEL HAND RAKE

STRAWBERRIES

CUCUMBER

BUMBLEBEE

TOMATOES

PLANT

APPLE

CARROTS

LETTUCE

FORK AND SPOON

TOY CAR

BREAD

CUTTING BOARD

STRAINER

TEAPOT

FRUIT

CUP

POT

OATMEAL COOKIES

DRAWING

PITCHER

APRON

TOWEL

CLOCK

DOG'S BOWLS

TOASTER

TRASH CAN

GLASS OF JUICE

GLASS OF WATER

SALT & PEPPER SHAKERS

LADLE

FRIED EGGS

PAN

FLAG

BICYCLE

STROLLER

BALL

LEAF

SHOVEL

BUCKET

BOOK

TOY TRUCK

TOY CAR

What time is it?

What is the boy drawing with chalk?

BLOCKS

DINOSAUR TOY

DOLL

TEAPOT

MODELING CLAY

ACTIVITY CUBE

CHALKBOARD

DOG

SNAKE

SHOPPING CART

POTATOES

CASH REGISTER

TOMATOES

PEARS

BANANAS

FRESH FISH

BASKET

FLOUR

ORANGES

BREAD

WALLET

MEAT

BERRY

YOGURT

SUGAR

EGGS

CUCUMBERS

CHEESE

PASTA

ORANGUTAN

MACAQUES

MACAW

BOA CONSTRICTOR

TURTLE

GORILLA

ICE-CREAM CART

TOUCAN

CHAMELEON

PARROT

COCKATOO

IGUANA

KIWI

ALLIGATOR

the sandcastle.

What things do you need for swimming?

BALL

SEAGULL

MASK AND SNORKEL

BEACH TOWEL

BEACH BAG

SWIM ARM BANDS

ICE CREAM

SWIMSUIT

SANDCASTLE

BOTTLE OF WATER

INFLATABLE RING